Juice Easy

Juicing Recipe Coloring Book

WRITTEN BY ROBERT NELSON HUMBERT

ILLUSTRATIONS BY LENA SEMENKOVA

Credits

Written By
Robert Nelson Humbert

Additional Recipes Provided By
Ashley Mcafee

Illustrations
Lena Semenkova

These recipes are from my
Houston Made Organic Plant Based
Beverage Brand Juice Easy.
Ashley & I are on a mission to make
Drinking Green & Thinking Green Cool
For Kids all over the world with this book.
So Parents enjoy making these delicious
Juice recipes and Kids have fun coloring
Inside or outside of the line as long as
You are creating together!

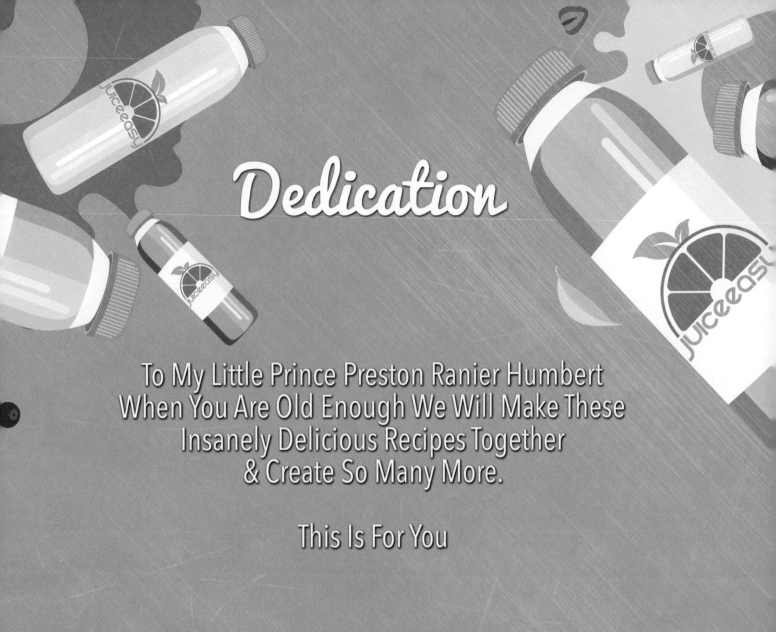

Dedication

To My Little Prince Preston Ranier Humbert
When You Are Old Enough We Will Make These
Insanely Delicious Recipes Together
& Create So Many More.

This Is For You

Juice Thoughts

Just Try Drinking Something
Green Today
Then Rinse & Repeat
Repetition
Always Defeats
Skepticism.

Great Greens

Ingredients:

SPINACH, KALE, CHARD, CELERY, CUCUMBER, APPLE, PINEAPPLE, LEMON, LIME, GINGER & TURMERIC

Great Greens

Recipe By Ashley Mcafee

Juice Each Ingredient
In Your Favorite Juicer in the Following Order

3 Cups Power Greens - Kale, Spinach & Chard
(Push Down with Cucumber)
1 Cucumber (Large)
2 Celery
4 Apples
3oz Pineapple
1/2oz Ginger
1/2oz Turmeric
1/2oz Lemon
1/2oz Lime
10oz of Spring & or Alkaline Water
Makes Three 12oz Glasses of Juice

Great Greens

Ingredients:

SPINACH, KALE, CHARD, CELERY, CUCUMBER, APPLE, PINEAPPLE, LEMON, LIME, GINGER & TURMERIC

Juice Thoughts

Squeeze The Day And
Get Ta Sippin.

Pink Paradise

Ingredients:

CARROT, PINEAPPLE, APPLE, BLACKBERRY, BLUEBERRY, STRAWBERRY, ORANGE, LEMON, LIME, GINGER & TURMERIC

Pink Paradise

Recipe By Ashley Mcafee

Juice Each Ingredient
In Your Favorite Juicer in the Following Order

15oz Carrot
1/4 Beet (For Pinkish Color)
5oz Blackberry (Measuered Un-Juiced)
5oz Blueberry (Measured Un-Juiced)
3oz Strawberry
1/2 Cucumber
1 Orange
5 Apples
3oz Pineapple
1/2oz Ginger
1/2oz Turmeric
1/2oz Lemon
1/2oz Lime
20oz of Spring & or Alkaline Water
Makes Five 12oz Glasses of Juce

Pink Paradise

Ingredients:

CARROT, PINEAPPLE, APPLE, BLACKBERRY, BLUEBERRY, STRAWBERRY, ORANGE, LEMON, LIME, GINGER & TURMERIC

Juice Thoughts

Expectations AreThe Roadmaps
To Greatness
May The Expectations
You Set For Yourself
Be High Enough For You To Reach
And Big Enough For You To Carry.

Human Beetbox

Ingredients:

BEETS, SPINACH, CELERY, PARSLEY,
PEARS, LEMON, LIME, GINGER & TURMERIC

Human BeetBox

Recipe By Robert Humbert

Juice Each Ingredient
In Your Favorite Juicer in the Following Order

5oz Red Beet
5oz Golden Beets
2 Cups Spinach (Measured Un-Juiced)
6 Celery
3 Stalks Parsley (Push with Pears)
4 Pears
1/2oz Ginger
1/2oz Turmeric
1/2oz Lemon
1/2oz Lime
Add 20oz of Spring & or Alkaline Water
Makes Five 12oz Glasses of Juce

Human Beetbox

Juice Cassy

Ingredients:

BEETS, SPINACH, CELERY, PARSLEY, PEARS, LEMON, LIME, GINGER & TURMERIC

Juice Thoughts

You Are What You Drink.

Refreshness

Ingredients:

PINEAPPLE, CUCUMBER, COCONUT WATER, MINT, LEMON, LIME, GINGER & TURMERIC

Refreshness

Recipe By Robert Humbert

Juice Each Ingredient
In Your Favorite Juicer in the Following Order

2 Cucumber (Large)
4 Apples
1 Pear
2oz Mint (Measure Un-Juiced)
4oz Pineapple (Juice with Mint)
1/2oz Ginger
1/2oz Turmeric
1/2oz Lemon
1/2oz Lime
5oz Coconut Water
Add 10oz of Spring & or Alkaline Water
Makes Four 12oz Glasses of Juce

Refreshness

Ingredients:

PINEAPPLE, CUCUMBER, COCONUT WATER, MINT, LEMON, LIME, GINGER & TURMERIC

Juice Thoughts

Try Giving Up One Thing You
Feel You Can't Live Without
For Just One Week
The Discipline & Self Control
You Will Gain From That
One Act of Submission
Will Prepare You For Any
Obstacales That May Come
Your Way.

Berry Delicious

Ingredients:

BEET, CARROT, BLACKBERRY, BLUEBERRY
STRAWBERRY, ORANGE, PINEAPPLE, APPLE
LEMON, LIME, GINGER & TURMERIC

Berry Delicious

Recipe By Ashley Mcafee

Juice Each Ingredient
- In Your Favorite Juicer in the Following Order

5oz Red Beet
10oz Carrot
5oz Blackberry (Measured Un-Juiced)
5oz Blueberry (Measured Un-Juiced)
3oz Strawberry
1 Orange (Small)
5 Apples
3oz Pineapple
1/2oz Ginger
1/2oz Turmeric
1/2oz Lemon
1/2oz Lime
20oz of Spring & or Alkaline Water
Makes Five 12oz Glasses of Juce

Berry Delicious

Ingredients:

BEET, CARROT, BLACKBERRY, BLUEBERRY
STRAWBERRY, ORANGE, PINEAPPLE, APPLE
LEMON, LIME, GINGER & TURMERIC

Juice Thoughts

Drink Green
Think Green.

Carrot Cake

Ingredients:

GOLDEN BEETS, CARROTS, KALE, APPLE, CINNAMON, LEMON, LIME, GINGER & TURMERIC

Carrot Cake

Recipe By Robert Humbert

Juice Each Ingredient
In Your Favorite Juicer in the Following Order

5oz Golden Beets
10oz Carrot
2 Cups Kale
4 Apples
30oz Pineapple
1/2 Teaspoon Cinnamon
1/2oz Ginger
1/2oz Turmeric
1/2oz Lemon
1/2oz Lime
Add 20oz of Spring & or Alkaline Water
Makes Four 12oz Glasses of Juce

Carrot Cake

Ingredients:

GOLDEN BEETS, CARROTS, KALE, APPLE, CINNAMON, LEMON, LIME, GINGER & TURMERIC

Juice Thoughts

When You Put Limits On
Youself You Are In Essence
Blocking Your Own Path
To Success
Be Limitless In Achieving
Your Goals
And Only Settle For
Greatness.

Parsnippy

Ingredients:

PARSNIP, APPLE, PEAR, SPINACH, COCONUT WATER, MINT, LEMON, LIME, GINGER & TURMERIC

Parsnippy

Recipe By Robert Humbert

Juice Each Ingredient
In Your Favorite Juicer in the Following Order
10oz Mint (Measured Un-Juiced)
3 Cups Spinach (Juice with Mint)
3 Whole Parsnip (Avg. Size)
3 Pears
4 Apples
1/2oz Ginger
1/2oz Turmeric
1/2oz Lemon
1/2oz Lime
5oz Coconut Water (No Pulp)
Add 10oz of Spring & or Alkaline Water
Makes Four 12oz Glasses of Juce

Parsnippy

Juice Easy

Ingredients:

PARSNIP, APPLE, PEAR, SPINACH, COCONUT WATER, MINT, LEMON, LIME, GINGER & TURMERIC

Juice Thoughts

Drink Like Your Life Depends On It.

Carrot Berry

Ingredients:

CARROT, STRAWBERRY, PINEAPPLE, APPLE, LEMON, TURMERIC & GINGER

Carrot Berry

Recipe By Ashley Mcafee

Juice Each Ingredient
In Your Favorite Juicer in the Following Order

15oz Carrot
3oz Strawberry
5 Apples
3oz Pineapple
1/2oz Ginger
1/2oz Turmeric
1/2oz Lemon
1/2oz Lime
20oz of Spring & or Alkaline Water
Makes Five 12oz Glasses of Juce

Carrot Berry

Ingredients:

CARROT, STRAWBERRY, PINEAPPLE, APPLE, LEMON, TURMERIC & GINGER

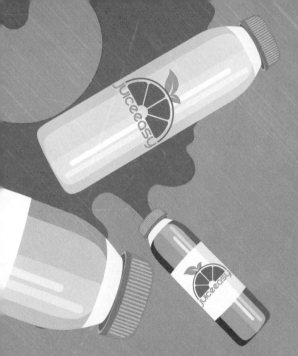

Archway Publishing books may be ordered through booksellers or by contacting:

Archway Publishing
1663 Liberty Drive
Bloomington, IN 47403
www.archwaypublishing.com
1 (888) 242-5904

Because of the dynamic nature of the Internet, any web addresses or links contained in this book may have changed since publication and may no longer be valid. The views expressed in this work are solely those of the author and do not necessarily reflect the views of the publisher, and the publisher hereby disclaims any responsibility for them.

Any people depicted in stock imagery provided by Getty Images are models, and such images are being used for illustrative purposes only.
Certain stock imagery © Getty Images.

Interior Image Credit: Lena Semenkova

ISBN: 978-1-4808-8224-9 (sc)
ISBN: 978-1-4808-8223-2 (e)

Print information available on the last page.

Archway Publishing rev. date: 10/11/2019

Printed in the United States
By Bookmasters